WORDS BY PSYCHE

APSARA

Made with ♥ on the Notion Press Platform
www.notionpress.com

Contents

Contents

Preface

This Book named Words by Psyche is a collection of poetry .It gives an idea about mother earth and nature.It also evokes curiosity and enlighten up the soul of readers. In this busy world ,no one has any time for anything .The aim of this book is to provide pure joy and happiness and a state of clamness along with relaxation. The world is evolving and so is the nature. It is experimental work and hope it touches your heart and mind of the readers.

1. Constellations in the sky

"

We are all like constellaions in the sky,

Unique and beautiful in our own ways

shines when our time is right "

2. How Beautiful our Earth is

The greeness of trees
puts everyone at ease
Crystal clear raindrops
makes everyone smile
while standing on the rooftop
Watching those bright sunsets
from the mountain top
makes life have no regrets
New hopes are brought
as the sun rises each days
The birds chirping reminds me
Giving me the feeling
of nostalgy of my childhood
Blooming of the flowers
removes the gloomness of life
Travelling across globe
brings new hope
as each day rises
Flying high in the sky
no more good days
no more sad days
Watch the sun rise in ectasy

spending time with family
and staying helathy
is what brings positivity

3. Grandpa

Wraping arms to hug you grandpa
now your wrapped in a white cloth
The medals I stare on your chest proudly
now its relaced with floral wreath sadly
You taught me to read the clock
now with tears I count the time left
The pciture of you and me on scooter
now your picture in a frame beside you lay
The song you sang for me
now there is prayer all around
You served the country
now the world is next to where you lay

4. Merry words

merry words flowing from my soul
you are reading them
with a smile you scroll
carry me to the world
where there is love
you are twirled
shabby all gone
with a smile you scroll
all tears gone by dawn
fairy tales with happy endings
is that's all that we want ?
with a smile you scroll
you are reading them

5. the wings

flying all i asked
while my wings shattered
inside the cage I stay

6. Do the world deserve it?

do the world deserve to hear these ?
"Better without you Who wouldn't be happy after an
upgrade
After going from a Maruti to a Mercedes
He's very loyal
But now it's time to upgrade
Time is irrelevant
He isn't happy with you anyway
Just leave him alone and let him be happy
I hope he breaks up with you
You do not deserve him
He is an amazing person
She's very hot She's so funny"
do the world deserve to hear these ?

7. Why give up?

I watched all of them betray me
Once again ,the same old story
put your emotions aside
that's what they said me
Trust is all gone aside
And Now I'm gone

8. Little did I know

Little did I know that
You went early to sleep
little did i know that
It was to meet her in midnight
Little did I know that
I am being played now
Little did I know that
You took picture for her
Little did I know
it was all at 2:16 AM
in the morning

9. Sound of silence

Where is sound of Silence ?
is it the brids chirping?
Or is when you carry a coffin?
Where is sound of Silence ?
Is it the love that you are searching ?
Or is it the baby's soft calling ?
Where is sound of Slience?
Is it the sun that's burning?
Or is it when the staring of dolphin?
Where is sound of Silence?
Is it the moon that's glowing ?
Or is it when the kid crawling?
Where is sound of Slience?
Is it the grass that's laying ?
Or is it when the roses are sprouting?
Where is sound of Silence ?
Is it the stars twinkling ?
Or when the natures calling ?

10. Adversity through harsdhips

cluster of roses
to envy friends my dear
thorns on my back
to save my dear
the crimson petals
to stand bright my dear
canes of roses
to hold you my dear
cluster of roses
to make you smile my dear
implanted below in vase
searching for my roots my dear

11. Can I?

Can I?

Can i ?

can I see the sunshine tomorrow ?

can I see the moonlight tomorrow ?

can I see the twinkling stars tomorrow ?

can I see the world tomorrow?

can I see the peace tomorrow?

can I see freedom tomorrow?

can I see acceptance tomorrow?

can I smile again tomorrow?

can I laugh with joy tomorrow

Can I?

Can I?

Chapter12

13. Soul did not forget

She wonder when the brown eyes be met
as the times ticking and ticking
emerald orchard where she swinging
her blooming face in the sunset
and the basket of kittens she pets
reminds her of the soft hair tickling
that plumpy lips she is thinking
all she knows her souls didn't forget

APSARA

14. Filter out

the cheeks blushing as the sun glowing
the bright pimples is it the stars in sky
the roots lay like silky hair hanging
the eyes sparkling and twinkling
the fingers as long as the snakes scales
the nails poking out for the knife
the feet stepped on the soil
the earth holds it from below
the nose shining at the constellation
the forehead as wide as a playground
the ears seen as snails crawls on ground
the arms floating as the branches of tree
for these is hidden by the filter

15. Spread your wings

The world's twirling
won't you dance along with it
the winds blowing
won't you sing along with it
the trees are crawling
won't you walk along with it
the sparrows chirping
won't you chatter with it
the falcons are up high in sky
won't you spread wings along with it
the fox lurking around
won't you join along with it
the world's twirling
won't you dance along with it
the winds blowing
won't you sing along with it
the trees crawling
won't you walk along with it
the falcons are up high in sky
won't you spread wings along with it?

16. Calling You

the winds calling out your name
how long will it take for you to hear it
sweetness of air flowing through
it's making you turn around
and walk through the field of greenery
it's petty simple to feel the sunshine
you are taking so much time to hear it
the arms carries the music
That it wishes to convey to you
the bags filled with secrets
that it wishes to convey to you
the breeze is following you
Turn around and it do no harm
for once just breathe it all out
as the winds calling out your name
all you have to do is
just hear the wind calling you

17. Look at you

Look at you
each time the branches gets crushed
each time you build the roots
each time you create new fruit
each time you try to survive the winds
each time you feel the air through
each time you see the breeze around you
each time you see the heaviness of leaves
each time you see the leaves fall down
each time your trunk is being cut
each time you endure the pain
each time you are calmed by mother earth each
time you empathised with creature
each time you cry with the rain
each time you are pulled from dark by sun
each time you are cared by the moon
each time you see the shooting stars
each time you get poured with the droplets
each time you are planted to
each time your journey comes to haitus
You are just getting stronger and stronger each time

18. Who is She?

She is full of thorns
But she is also the friendly
She has the softest heart
but she is also the mighty
She is looking like a art
but she is also the fancy
She has an bright aura
but she is also the lucky
She is not any weak
but she is also the opportunity
She is carrying her dreams
but she is also the pretty
She is planted in a pot
but she is also the beauty

19. The river that flows

The river that flows
like the tear drop the falls
it greets the trees around
like the widening of eyeballs
it changes the direction
like the pupil moves sideways
it flows as sweet as ice
like the salty tear drops falls
it is given different names
like the different shades it glows
It sometimes entered the home
like the vision it provides
the river that flows
like the starlight that shows

20. What are we?

We were like the sun and moon
brighting up each others day
lightning up each others lifes
yet you went for a brighter one
while I provided my light throughout
the laughter and cries
all that sky replays
for all I remember is your bright smile
you went for a star a pretty one
while I provided my care through the dark
the fire ignited all along the way
while I provided my care through out
you taught me a lesson all the way
to not touch fire as the sun shines bright

21. Me and the moon

me and the moon
are like best friends
got pulled to the light
when almost drowned
in my own thoughts
gave the very comfort
as it was all alone
moon smiles at me
me and the moon
are like best friends

22. Beauty of family

watching the sun goes down to her home
removing the hair below the sea
it hangs down showing its length
and after a while the dusk fills in
her small kids enter the galaxy
they shine through out bright
the elderly white figure watches them
smiling brightly and talking about the kids
and from distance sun takes a small nap

23. The night has arrived

the night has arrived
oh ! what do you see ?
waiting ,the life smiles
what is there left
the heavens calls
oh ! what do you see?
your name ,is what
said the misery gone
the silence world peace
oh ! what do you see?
the pigeons, is what flies
all voice will be heard
the cold night calms down
oh ! what do you see ?
the breeze ,is what draws
warmth will be felt
the night has arrived
oh ! what do you see ?
the life ,that waits for you
all will be happy and lucky

24. The night that we met

solitude in the amidst
the twinkling shines
souls that convinced
if the stars could speak
gratitude you will keep
feel it may weight ton
adored by the milky way
below which we wait
under the moonlight
that's the night that
we both met

25. My friend

speaks your mind
through all the whistles
jumping through the water

"how fascinating to jump like that!"
was all that you were asked
"as fascinating as feet touches ground"
was all that you replied while
you only stay lows from
the predator of the deep
"yes you guessed it right
i am the so called dolphins "

26. Spring

spring is when flowers blooms
removes ,all negative and glooms
fields be filled with petals
and not ,just the battles
brids be chirping happy again
out of their, broken cages in rain
the daylight pierce through the trees
as the worries , gone through breeze
mornings be brighter and adored
no more diseases, like before

27. Autumn

The crawling of the feet
Oh! is in autumn
the giggling is more sweet
Oh in the autumn
leaning in of arms
Oh! is in autumn
running on farms
Oh! is in autumn
Sleeping like a bear
Oh! is in autumn
All that is care
Oh! is in autumn
keep her safe it's autumn
after all being a child is awesome

28. Picture

pretty you smile in the pictures
every minute that counts
words flowing like the dandelions
eyes flattering as moving through daisies
lips widened like the pulling of ropes
as you wander in the morning light
pretty you smile in the pictures
every minute that counts
words flowing like the dandelions
eyes flattering as moving through daisies
lips widened like the pulling of ropes
as you wander in the morning light

29. Keep guessing

It's January
and yet somedays it's red
some days it's white
ome days it's orange
some says it's pastel
when it gets heavy
those days it's dripping tears
the mood is warm
or cold ,as freezing
maybe even flowery
yet you can keep guessing
what it is about

30. The mountains

as pointy as the finger nails
some of them broken and fallen down
enormously for the sight
as danger to the roads
the path is blocked by the pieces
sometimes in different shapes
standing with fierce courage
while we go through or nearby it
as the moonlight shines
souls brighten up
the world's not empty anymore
get up and go running down
along with the foxes
and pray that you will win
encourage more
let the light brighten up
not just yours but others day also

The End

Words aren't enough to express my gratitude to the readers .Thank you for choosing to read this book as a enthusiastic reader ,I've always wondered what is it is like to publish something and this is a poetry book this book contains 30 poems which was written in the concept for the mother earth.